The Bond

Succeeding in Sales and Unlocking
the Power of Relationship Building

Sandra Rojas

The Bond
Author: Sandra Rojas
Editing and Proofreading Services: Luke Palder
Graphic Designer: Rafael Orellana
Published by: UnilX LLC
Copyright © 2025 Sandra Rojas
ISBN: 979-8-9927212-0-1

All rights reserved. No part of this publication may be reproduced, stored in a retrieval system, or transmitted in any form or by any means, electronic, mechanical, photocopying, recording, or otherwise, without the prior permission of the copyright owner.
First published 2025.

Contents

Introduction	5
Chapter 1 Understanding the Power of Listening in Sales	15
Chapter 2 Properly Qualifying Opportunities	27
Chapter 3 From Identifying Pain Points and Challenges to Customizing the Perfect Offer	41
Chapter 4 The Role of Relationship Building	57
Chapter 5 Effective Communication Strategies	71
Chapter 6 Building a Healthy Pipeline: The Key to Sustainable Sales Success	97
Chapter 7 From Overcoming Challenges in Consultative Sales to Building Long-Term Relationships	117
Chapter 8 Closing	127
Chapter 9 What Makes You Good	141
Chapter 10 What Makes You Unique	149
Appendix 1 Answers to Exercises	159
Appendix 2 Practical Applications of Consultation	162

Introduction

Officially, I've been in sales for over 15 years, but if you ask me, it feels like I've been selling forever. The first real cold sales experience I remember was when I was 12; I decided to sell tours during the summer. While my mom was shopping at the mall, I ventured into a tour operator and inquired about the prices for every single tour they offered. At the end of my questioning, I asked, "If I bring you clients, how much would you discount those prices so I can make some money too?" Of course, they all laughed, but they answered me, though I couldn't tell if it was out of curiosity to see if I could bring someone in or if it was just to get rid of the little girl bugging them.

Anyway, they offered me a special price and shared the discounted values.

I went home, looked at the options, picked two tours, and prepared to sell them. Armed with markers, cardboard, paper, scissors, tape (no printer or social media available at the time), and a receipt book, I was confident I would make some sales.

My family used to live in a building in the tourist area of Santa Marta, a beautiful city on the Colombian Caribbean coast. On my first day, I eagerly offered tours to all the tourists in my building. Some people smiled and let me talk for a while, while others asked questions that were more about my motives for doing this "job" than about the tours themselves. Disappointed, I learned my first hard lesson: many people would say "no." But I wasn't going to give up. In the days that followed, I visited different places—the beach, the pool area, the game area—and did the same.

I started noticing something interesting. When I began by presenting the plans, people often asked questions I didn't want them to. So, I shifted my approach to start conversations by asking them about their vacations—what they had done and what they were looking forward to. Interestingly, when they expressed interest in local places, I offered to "get the plan for them." That's how my first business began; I sold my first tours!

With the joy of my first independent income came my second lesson: if you persist and improve your strategy, after many "no" responses, you'll eventually get your "yes." And although I didn't realize it at the time, I can now see a third lesson: if you focus the conversation on yourself or your product, the client will steer the discussion their way;

however, if you make the client the center of the conversation, you'll have the opportunity to guide the path toward what interests you.

I believe that in life, we each have what moves us—our passions and the things we are good at. In my case, I know I'm good at sales because the numbers have proven it; however, I'm passionate about education and technology, as I truly believe these are the tools that can shape the world and improve people's lives. Several years ago, I decided to make the most of both by working in education, technology, and, naturally, educational technology, primarily in the sales area.

This book was born from an initiative to merge my two worlds. As someone I love very much said when he read the first draft of my manuscript, "This is a book that wanted to be a sales manual." I can't promise you an adventurous thriller or an inspiring novel;

rather, this is simply the book I wish I had read when I was just starting out in sales or the first time I had to lead a sales team. It may not be a romance novel, but after reading it, you just might be able to write your own "happily ever after."

There's no shortage of sales literature out there, packed with theories, old quotes, and success stories that are more inspiring than instructional. This book, however, rather than aiming to impress with a personal tale of triumphs or glories, seeks to be a practical guide rooted in real-world experience, offering actionable tips drawn from over 15 years of commercial growth. Inside, you'll find not just lessons learned from mistakes made, challenges overcome, and obstacles faced but also the insights that have driven real sales success.

In the world of sales, there's often an emphasis on closing deals and achieving short-term success. However, the true power of sales lies not in one-time transactions but in the art of building long-term relationships with clients. This book explores the importance of shifting our focus from immediate gains to cultivating long-lasting connections, and how this approach can revolutionize the way we drive sales.

In today's fast-paced business environment, it's easy to fall into the trap of chasing after quick wins and closing against the clock. The allure of closing a deal and achieving immediate success can be tempting, but it often comes at the expense of long-term growth. One-time transactions may provide a temporary boost, but they lack the depth and sustainability that comes with building lasting relationships.

At the heart of successful long-term relationship building is a foundation of trust and loyalty.

When clients trust us and feel understood, heard, and cared for, they are more likely to remain loyal and continue doing business with us over time, expand their business, and eventually refer us to new clients. Trust is not built overnight; it is nurtured through consistent delivery of value—from proposal to implementation—open communication, and a genuine commitment to the client's success. By prioritizing trust and loyalty, we create a solid framework for sustained growth and mutual benefit.

Long-term relationship building requires a deep understanding of our clients' needs, goals, financial capabilities, and challenges. By taking the time to truly listen and comprehend their unique circumstances, we can tailor our solutions to meet their specific requirements. This level of customization not only enhances the client's experience but also positions us as trusted advisors who are invested in their long-term success.

One of the most compelling advantages of focusing on long-term relationship building is the potential for repeat business and referrals. When clients are satisfied with our products or services, they are more likely to return for future engagements. Furthermore, they become the best advocates who refer us to their network, expanding our reach and opening doors to new opportunities. This virtuous cycle of repeat business and referrals is a testament to the power of long-term relationships.

Building long-term relationships requires a strategic approach. This book explores various strategies and techniques that can be employed to foster meaningful connections with clients. From proactive communication to personalized follow-ups, we delve into practical steps that can be taken to nurture relationships and create a solid foundation for continued success.

In a world that often prioritizes short-term gains, choosing long-term relationship building in sales is a paradigm shift that can yield remarkable results. By shifting our focus from one-time transactions to cultivating lasting connections, we unlock the true potential of sales. This book aims to guide you on this transformative journey, equipping you with the insights and tools to build authentic, enduring relationships that will drive your success in the ever-evolving world of sales.

Stop being just a supplier, and become the partner that every client wishes to have.

Chapter 1

Understanding the Power of Listening in Sales

It is well known that speaking a lot is a characteristic possessed by many sales representatives, though most would rather not admit it. Nevertheless, the traditional peddler who speaks to convince and says anything to make a person buy—even if it means running away from town—must be left behind.

Companies and buying behaviors have evolved, and so have the people making the purchasing decisions. As a result, we must evolve too.

You may have heard the term "consultative sales," but what does it mean? Consultative sales refers to a sales approach that focuses on understanding and solving a customer's specific needs through expert or informed advice, from which tailored solutions are provided. In other words, unlike traditional sales, it does not prioritize simply selling a product or service. On the contrary, it emphasizes building a relationship with the client by acting as a trusted advisor, which ultimately leads to increased and repeat sales.

In consultative sales, the ability to truly listen to clients is a skill that sets the exceptional apart from the average. Listening is not just about hearing words; it's about understanding the underlying needs, desires, and challenges of the client. This chapter explores the importance of engaging in active listening, developing empathy, uncovering hidden needs, and building trust through effective listening.

The Importance of Active Listening

Effective communication begins with active listening. Active listening involves fully engaging with the client by paying attention to their words, tone, and body language. It requires setting aside personal biases and distractions to focus solely on the client's message—not just the words they say, but also the missing pieces of the puzzle (the tone, content, and even the unspoken elements) that can help you identify the "right questions" to ask during the conversation. By actively listening, consultants can gain valuable insights into the client's perspective, needs, and expectations.

- Don't forget to arrive in neutral gear...

To truly understand a client's needs, it's essential to approach conversations with an open mind and refrain from making assumptions. This is one of the most difficult and least common skills in sales, but it's perhaps the most important foundation for building a long-term relationship with a client.

I have always said, "A proper consultation leads to the right offer; the right offer leads to a well-sold deal; and a well-sold deal results in a well-implemented project that leads to renewals and grows over time."

I recall a junior sales executive at a software company who had a first meeting with a major university in Peru. Before arriving at the meeting, he had assumed that the institution had a limited budget for each student based on its location and the number of students they were purchasing for. Acting on this assumption, he sent a full product presentation to the client before even listening to them. Then, he started the meeting by "convincing" them of the solution he had already chosen. The prospect listened and decided to send the proposal for internal review. After a 30-day delay in receiving a response from the university, I decided to attend the next meeting. We began by listening to their feedback on the offer and their actual needs. It quickly became clear that the proposal didn't align with their expectations. I started asking questions and actively listening as if it were the very first meeting. The result: they needed a completely different solution—a higher-tier option from the catalog —and were willing to pay for it as long as it addressed their pain points.

Pre-assumptions often lead to mistakes, and, more often than not, those mistakes work against us.

Do not sacrifice a client who could become a long-term customer by pushing them into a one-time purchase of something they don't need.

Know your catalog by heart, but don't arrive at the meeting with your client armed only with a 50-page brochure filled with hundreds of products or services. Start by creating an environment of trust; ask the right questions, and listen carefully in a warm, conversational manner. Pay attention not only to the words but also to the emphasis, emotions, and nonverbal cues of your client. Listen more than you talk, and never interrupt.

Active listening involves giving your undivided attention, asking clarifying questions, and focusing 100% solely on the client. By doing so, you will gain valuable insights into the client's goals, preferences, timeline, budget, and pain points. This information will help you determine whether an opportunity exists and, if so, will be key to shaping your proposal.

- Conducting Live Active Research

While actively listening to clients, it's important to conduct live research to gather real-time information. This can involve taking notes on specific points related to the types of projects you sell.

Building a strong proposal is crucial during the sales process, but even before reaching that step, you need to determine whether it's worth investing your time and resources in the negotiation. You must assess whether it's a potential deal or just a curious prospect inquiring about prices or passing by. This is why gathering the right information to recognize and qualify the opportunity is essential.

We will revisit how to qualify an opportunity later in the book.

- Developing Empathy for the Client

Empathy is a crucial trait for successful consultative sales professionals. It involves putting yourself in the client's shoes, understanding their emotions, and seeing the world from their perspective. Developing empathy allows consultants to connect with clients on a deeper level, fostering trust and building long-lasting relationships.

Empathizing does not always mean agreeing; it means understanding the client's perspective and the circumstances from which they are experiencing a situation. It may not solve the problem, but it can provide the right perspective to propose practical and achievable alternatives for both the provider and the client.

- Uncovering Hidden Needs Through Confirming the Context and What You Hear

Clients often have needs that they may not explicitly express. Listening carefully enables consultants to uncover these hidden needs by asking confirming or probing questions and paying attention to subtle cues. Don't be afraid to ask or paraphrase, such as: "From what you're telling me, I understand... Is that correct?"; "Does that mean that...? Am I wrong?"; "What alternatives have you considered for...?"; "What's the goal of the program you're planning to launch?"

By actively seeking to understand the client's challenges and aspirations, consultants can provide tailored solutions that address their unspoken needs. You may gather the information you need, and your client or prospect may end up adjusting their expectations to better align with their actual means and/or budget.

- Building Trust

Trust is the foundation of any successful client–consultant relationship. I believe it starts with a conversation, continues with a consultation, and, if done right and consistently, develops into a lasting relationship.

Listening attentively and showing a genuine interest in the client's concerns and goals helps build trust. When clients feel heard and understood, they are more likely to trust the consultant's advice and recommendations. Trust leads to stronger partnerships, increased client loyalty, and, ultimately, more successful sales.

Do not abuse the trust given to you by exploiting the client's wallet unnecessarily. Offer valuable projects and grow your sales by providing options that positively impact your client according to their own goals.

* * *

Practical Tips for Improving Listening Skills:

Improving listening skills is an ongoing process that requires practice and self-awareness.

- *Arrive without preconceptions*
- *Maintain eye contact*
- *Paraphrase to ensure understanding*
- *Avoid interrupting the client*
- *Give 100% undivided attention*

Chapter 2

Properly Qualifying Opportunities

Recognizing and Qualifying Opportunities

In addition to understanding pain points, it is equally important to recognize potential opportunities. By identifying gaps in the client's current services, tools, or offerings along with their internal timelines and processes, sales professionals can present tailored solutions that meet specific needs. This requires a deep understanding of the client's industry, competitors, and market trends. However, even before considering making an offer, we must first ask ourselves whether or not there is an opportunity in front of us.

It is commonly stated, "We create the opportunities; you can sell to anyone." In my opinion, we salespeople identify opportunities. Marketing can work with us to better understand our target clients and help with earlier stages, but our role as sales representatives is to clearly determine whether an opportunity exists and whether it can realistically be worked toward a deal closure within a defined period.

Objectifying the Process

I don't even remember when I first heard the term, but some colleagues and I have been using it for a long time now. We call it "Sugar Ears" when salespeople hear what they want to hear instead of what the client is actually saying. Sadly, it is a common condition among sales consultants who are anxious to close deals. We have all seen opportunities in the pipeline that last for months, even years, without real movement or development. Yet, the opportunity owner always finds an excuse, saying, "They are about to close the deal" or "I know they are going to buy." In the end, this practice leads to unrealistic pipeline forecasts and wasted time.

While there are hundreds of techniques to qualify leads and deals, from BANT (Budget, Authority, Need, Timing) Scoring to CHAMP (Challenges, Authority, Money, Prioritization) Scoring, and from GPCTBA/C&I (Goals, Plans, Challenges, Timeline, Budget, Authority, and Consequences/Implications) to Lead Scoring based on demographics and behavioral data. I honestly don't think there is a single, one-size-fits-all sales methodology for qualifying your prospects. You may find your best fit—or even create your own—as you progress, depending on your product, service, industry, and the lessons learned from your professional maturity and successful experiences.

In the meantime, I'll share the approach I prefer. I like using numbers to "let the math tell me whether or not there is an opportunity," and if there is, how important it should be considered within my pipeline.

- How does it work?

The first step of qualifying an opportunity is taking into consideration five core factors:

- Deal size
- Decision-Maker
- Need
- Time
- Budget

Deal size: How large is the potential sale you are qualifying compared with your ideal deal size?

You should have an "ideal deal size" as a reference according to your market, product, and prices. Example: One company could have an ideal deal size of 12 dozens of product per purchase order, while another could have 100 unit licenses per order.

Decision-Maker: Is your contact the decision-maker, a power sponsor, an sponsor, an influencer, or how likely is it that this person will introduce you to the purchaser?

Need: Is the purchase of your product vital for your prospect? Is there any consequence for the non-purchase, or would they need to buy it from your competence to avoid those consequences?

Time: Is there a defined timeline for the project in the short-medium term?

Budget: Does the client have a budget assigned for the project? Is that amount enough to pay for the solution you can offer to cover their need?

- How to Score

All this information should be gathered as part of the conversation when we are listening to the client or prospect, asking the right questions, and taking notes. Remember, it's a consultant conversation that is expected to be stress-free and enjoyable; don't make it a quiz or an interview. Use your charm and professionalism to make the client comfortable enough to express themselves.

For the qualification to be successful, the "answer" to those questions MUST come from information provided by the client source and NEVER through guesswork, intuition, or assumption.

Every mentioned criterion should be punctuated with a number from 1 to 5, with 5 being the best possible scenario and 1 the worst.

Remember, it is important to make the qualification as objective as possible, so it should be based on the information given by the client and not on personal assumptions.

• What each score means:

5: It is your best possible scenario.

4: It is not ideal but fairly positive.
E.g.:
-You achieve at least 50% of your ideal deal size.
-Your point of contact may not be the only decision-maker but is one of them or takes part in the decision-making process directly.

-Not purchasing the solution you offer may not lead to negative consequences for the client, but they expressed an honest interest in it, and the project is considered vital or is already planned for their organization.

-There may not be an urgency for the immediate acquisition of the solution, but it is expected to be acquired during the current quarter (or sales period, depending on the industry).

-The client does not have a budget that is enough to pay for the solution you can offer to cover their need but is close enough (75–80%)

3: This score is only for when the information was not given or was unknown by the point of contact spoken with.

When the answer to any of the mentioned facts is "I don't know," 3 is the value to be used as neutral qualification, to be adjusted during the negotiations once you receive the information from the prospect.

2: It is not a good scenario but is not the worst. E.g.:

-You achieve at least 5% of your ideal deal size.

-Your point of contact may not be a decision-maker but gets you close to whoever is for an introduction or a recommendation.

-There is no need for the solution but expressed interest.

-Their buying intentions are up to six months from the moment of contact (or after the next sales period, depending on the industry).

-The client has a budget that is 50% of the price for the solution you can offer to cover their need, or you may need to offer a substitute, sacrificing key conditions from the client's request. Or, not having an assigned budget, they positively express that they may be able to get some funds.

1. It is the worst scenario.

E.g.:

-The deal size is less than 5% of your ideal size.

-Your point of contact is far away from and unrelated to any decision-maker.

-There is no need for the solution, and while they are willing to hear you, they have not expressed explicit interest.

-Their buying intentions are more than six months from the moment of contact.

-The client has a budget that is insignificant for any solution you can offer to cover their need, or part of it. Or, having confirmed that there is a positive general budget, they can't confirm if it will be allocated to cover the project in any proportion.

0: If you consider that any of the criteria should be 0 because there is not an existent resource, do not bother to tabulate; you do not have an opportunity.

The valuation of your opportunity will be the total of the 5 criteria scores, as follows:

20 or more: This means you could have an ideal client. It's where you need to spend most of your time and efforts because it's almost certainly a sale.

13 or more: This means you have an opportunity.

12 or less: This means you could probably have an opportunity at another moment, but unfortunately right now there is NO opportunity. Discard the prospect from your pipeline, and if you have a marketing department, assign it to them for nurture and campaigns that could contribute to generating a future opportunity.

* * *

Practical Exercises to better understand how to qualify an opportunity: Take a pencil and score each case according to the given information.

You are a software distributor, and your ideal deal size is 5,000 units per purchase order.

Case A

Fact	Situation	Score
Size (DS)	Private university interested in 5,000 licenses	
Decision-Maker (DM)	Procurement department	
Need (N)	They are actively looking for licenses for their campus computers	
Time (T)	They need them to be installed in less than two months	
Budget (B)	There is a budget, but it is still unknown	
TOTAL		

Case B

Fact	Situation	Score
Size (DS)	Company with 80 computers	
Decision-Maker (DM)	Receptionist	
Need (N)	We offer the software, and they seem to be interested	
Time (T)	They do not have a clear purchasing date, but it may be in a year	
Budget (B)	They do not have an assigned budget for the project, but it was said that they may take it from something else	
TOTAL		

Chapter 3

From Identifying Pain Points and Challenges to Customizing the Perfect Offer

One of the primary objectives of analyzing client needs is to identify the pain points and challenges they face. By understanding and empathizing with their struggles or gaps, sales professionals can position their products or services as solutions. This requires probing questions, careful observation, and the ability to connect the dots between the client's needs and the offerings available.

We all have heard the statement "knowledge is power," and in the world of sales, that meaning can take on a bold dimension. Understanding your product portfolio is crucial for providing tailored advice to potential clients. As sales professionals, we are tasked with guiding our clients toward the right solutions that meet their needs.

However, without a deep understanding of our product offerings, our recommendations may fall flat. In this chapter, we will explore the importance of knowing your product portfolio and how this enables us to customize solutions, offer expert recommendations, balance short-term and long-term goals, and present realistic options to potential clients.

Customizing Solutions to Meet Client Needs

Knowing the ins and outs of your product portfolio allows you to customize solutions that meet the unique needs of potential clients. Each customer has specific requirements, preferences, and pain points. By delving into the details of your product offerings, you gain a comprehensive understanding of how each product addresses different customer needs.

Armed with this knowledge, you can provide personalized solutions that align with their specific requirements, ensuring that you are offering the right product at the right time.

We love having a lot to offer and to choose from. Nevertheless, the bigger the portfolio, the bigger the challenge.

How to Properly Know Your Portfolio

The most frequent question regarding portfolio knowledge is about memory. Mistaking memory for knowledge is something understandable due to the way old-fashioned schools taught many of us when we were young. But far from what people may think, the importance of portfolio knowledge resides in how well you understand each product and where it sits in the map of your organization.

When training my sales teams, I follow at least three fundamental steps to ensure they understand what we have to offer to the market:

If you are a sales representative, gather the information and seek help when needed to follow the steps.

If you are a leader, making sure this process is successful will save you money, time, and effort in individual process development and assistance regarding product comprehension.

Step 1:
- Present, show, and explain to your team product by product.
- Let them study them one by one.
- Encourage them to create a 30-second elevator speech for each product; that way, you can make sure they know it by heart.

The elevator speech is not just any piece of information; it has to be fully organized to ensure that the person who listens to it fully understands the core of your product. This means at least what it does, who it's intended for, and what makes it unique.

Of course, order is important to make it easier for the prospects or clients to "draw" your product or service in their minds. Organize each speech from the general to the detailed information, starting with an "overall" and ending with specific characteristics that are worthy of being highlighted.

Once you (or your team if you are a leader) have championed the speeches for all your portfolio products, separately, you need to make sure they "sit" in the right place in the market they are intended for. To do this, you need to understand and make sure your team understands your market.

Step 2:
Analyze and understand your buyer persona and your product market. How is it divided up? Do you have a main market and a secondary one? Do you divide your market geographically or by client type? Do you have restrictions of your products in certain markets or different versions of them accordingly?

Create the questions that you must answer to be able to properly advise the client.

A "buyer persona" is a semi-fictional representation of an ideal customer based on market research and real data about existing customers. Buyer personas are created to help businesses understand their target audience better, including their demographics, behaviors, interests, pain points, and buying patterns.

I recommend you to develop a detailed buyer persona, or personas if you have more than one target audience, so that your company can tailor its marketing and sales strategies to effectively reach and engage with your target customers.

This approach will allow you to create more personalized and targeted campaigns, products, and services that resonate with your audience, ultimately leading to increased sales and customer satisfaction. Buyer personas are a valuable tool for you to align the marketing and sales efforts of your organization with the needs and preferences of your target customers.

You need to fully understand who buys your products, what they do, where they go, and, for sure, where they buy them.

After understanding your market and segments, place every product in the corresponding segment, even with variations.

Build your own mental map for the product portfolio within a structure that reflects clearly and accurately your market and segments. Sit each product where it belongs according to their target market, needs, capabilities, restrictions and advantages. To make sure it is done properly, use your "must" questions to turn it into a decision tree.

Step 3:

Practice offering expert recommendations on two levels: with a formal, professional note, and with a casual, personal recommendation tone.

Remember, people don't like hosting sales representatives that pressure them to buy; they buy on the successful recommendation of a trusted advisor, whether it is a friend, family member, or someone they believe is qualified to provide counsel.

They also buy for emotion, aspirational scenery, a heartfelt mission, an idealistic investment. Or they buy for a tangible need, when there is a situation in the medium term or near future that may benefit from a purchase decision in the present.

Use case studies and role-plays to emulate the characteristics and moments of real clients to practice and bulletproof your decision tree and your 30-second speeches.

By analyzing the features, benefits, and limitations of each product, you can provide insights that go beyond generic advice. This expertise allows you to guide potential clients toward the products that best suit their needs, ensuring that they receive the maximum value from their purchase.

Knowing your product portfolio inside out enables you to make informed decisions and provide recommendations that are tailored to each customer's unique situation.

While asking the right questions and listening to your prospect, you will be able to navigate in your head through your own decision tree, being able to realize the solutions from your portfolio that "naturally" fit your client's needs.

A big mistake of many organizations is thinking that offering a long list of products or a huge catalog to the client will make them sell more. What I have found during the last decade is that there is a lot of truth in the paradox of choice.

The paradox of choice explains why sometimes less is more. While it's true that human beings are happier when they have the freedom of choice, it's also true that having too many options, instead of bringing happiness, creates anxiety and will leave the client less satisfied with the decision that is made.

The reason? When too many options are on the table and the client picks one, instead of being able to gather all the wins from the choice that was made, they will remain with the feeling of what could have been or the opportunity that was lost from not picking a different one.

Does this mean that you need to have a really small portfolio? If you were in an exclusive restaurant, maybe I would suggest having a relatively small menu that rotates with a certain frequency. But talking about consultant sales for products or services, which I think most of you are involved with, the solution doesn't reside in cutting down the options that exist in the portfolio; it's more about presenting to the client only those that are truly relevant for their current needs, according to what we have gathered from listening to our client and asking the right questions (following our product decision tree).

In other words, instead of presenting a 300-page catalog of ice cream flavors, I offer my clients what I consider the "vanilla, strawberry, and chocolate" of our products in relation to their reality. That way, they will have the freedom to choose, and I can make sure their choice is aligned with what could solve their problem, will make them happy, and/or is achievable according to their budget.

Balancing Short-Term and Long-Term Goals

One of the key challenges in sales is striking a balance between short-term and long-term goals. While it may be tempting to focus solely on immediate sales, a successful salesperson understands the importance of building long-term relationships. By knowing your product portfolio, you can identify the products that cater to both short-term needs and long-term aspirations. This balanced approach ensures that potential clients receive the right solutions for their immediate requirements while also considering their future growth and expansion plans.

Presenting Realistic Options

Knowing your product portfolio enables you to present realistic options to potential clients. By understanding the features, pricing, and capabilities of each product, you can recommend solutions that align with their budget, requirements, and expectations.

This tailored approach ensures that potential clients have a clear understanding of the available options and can make informed decisions based on realistic outcome expectations. By presenting options that align with your product portfolio, you build trust and confidence in your recommendations.

Knowing your product portfolio and having that knowledge organized in a usable way is the foundation for providing tailored advice to potential clients. It allows you to customize solutions, offer expert recommendations, balance short-term and long-term goals, and present realistic options.

By delving into the intricacies of your product offerings, you gain a comprehensive understanding of how each product addresses different customer needs.

As sales professionals, it is our duty to harness the power of this knowledge and provide advice that is truly tailored to each potential client's unique circumstances and reality. By doing so, we increase our chances of success and build long-lasting relationships with our customers.

By adopting a client-centric approach, actively listening, conducting live research, identifying pain points and challenges, recognizing opportunities, and gathering data and feedback, we can position ourselves as trusted advisors and provide tailored solutions that meet our clients' needs.

By consistently refining our understanding of client needs, market conditions, product updates, and portfolio advantages and limitations, sales professionals can stay ahead of the competition and drive business growth.

Chapter 4

The Role of Relationship Building

In today's fast-paced, competitive market, it's easy to forget one of the most powerful assets a business can have: strong, lasting relationships with clients. While it's essential to bring in new business, it's the ongoing, repeat relationships that truly sustain a company's growth and reputation. These relationships are the foundation of long-term success, and they are built on trust, communication, and a genuine commitment to the client's needs.

At the heart of any great relationship is trust. Trust is the glue that holds everything together. When your clients trust you, they are more likely to stay loyal to your brand, purchase from you repeatedly, continue doing business with you over the long term, and recommend you to others.

But trust doesn't happen overnight—it's earned through consistent, transparent communication, delivering on promises, and truly showing you care about the client's goals. Trust is about being reliable, following through on your word, and demonstrating that you're always looking out for your client's best interests.

A Two-Way Street

In the digital age, it's easy to get caught up in email chains, automated messages, or even social media. While these are useful tools for communication, they don't build relationships. Relationships are built through genuine, human connection. As a sales professional, it's your job to move beyond the one-way flow of information. Yes, emails can help with sharing details, sending quotes, or introducing a product—but they don't foster the deeper connection that leads to long-term partnerships.

To build a bond, you need to listen and be listened to, to empathize and elicit sympathy, to show you care and establish confidence links. So, pick up the phone, make that call, and go the extra mile to truly connect with your client. Get your keys and drive to that office, invite that person to have a coffee or go to that event (yes, even the ones that seem "boring" or "irrelevant"), and make it interesting getting to know your clients deeper than you do now.

These personal touches show your commitment to the relationship and give you the chance to listen deeply—to understand not just their business needs but their personal goals, their challenges, and their aspirations.

When you can transform a business relationship into a personal connection, it becomes harder for a buyer to switch suppliers. It's easy for a buyer to change a supplier; it's difficult for a person to break their relationship with a good partner and friend. They're not just working with a vendor—they're working with a trusted partner and a friend. And that makes all the difference.

Understanding Your Client's Needs: The Power of Personalization

Great relationships start with understanding—and I mean a deep, meaningful understanding. Yes, it's essential to know what products or services a client needs, but that's only the surface. There are a whole lot of "unspoken" conditions that matter in a deal—nuances that could impact the client's buying decision and their satisfaction in the long run. For example, the tone of an email request or the urgency of a problem may tell you more than what's written in the official procurement documents.

To truly serve your client, you need to go beyond the obvious. Get to know your client on a personal level. What are their goals, not just for today, but for the future? What challenges are they facing that they may not even be sharing with you yet?

By actively listening, observing, and asking the right questions, you'll uncover these "unspoken" needs, which will allow you to offer products or services that are not only relevant but also deeply aligned with what the client actually needs.

This level of personalized attention shows your client that no one understands them better than you—and no one cares as much as you do. When you invest in learning what matters most to your clients, you build customer loyalty and retention in a way that's hard to match. People don't just want to buy products or services—they want to feel understood, valued, and respected. This kind of attention to detail transforms a simple transaction into a long-term partnership.

Consistency Is Key

As you build a relationship with your clients, you must remember that consistent communication is crucial. The strongest relationships are not built on occasional check-ins or sporadic sales calls. Rather, it's the ongoing dialogue that keeps you top of mind and keeps the relationship healthy. It also provides an opportunity to address any issues or concerns promptly, showing clients that their satisfaction is a top priority.

Don't fall into the trap of only reaching out when you need something. The worst thing you can do is become the "money grabber" who only calls when it's time to renew contracts or ask for a purchase. Be proactive in your communication. Check in with your clients even when they're not actively buying from you. A simple "How's the project going?"

or "Congrats on the promotion!" can go a long way in building rapport and trust.

Remember, it's not about bombarding your clients with constant emails or phone calls. It's about meaningful touch points throughout the year—whether it's to acknowledge their accomplishments, ask how their needs have changed, or simply wish them well during the holidays. These small gestures show you're thinking of them, not just as clients but as real people with evolving needs.

Delivering Value: Going Beyond Expectations

The foundation of any great relationship is the value you provide. But here's the catch: it's not just about meeting expectations—it's about exceeding them. Delivering on your promises is important, but delivering more than expected is what separates the good salespeople from the great ones.

When you consistently deliver high-quality products or services, and you show your client that you are genuinely invested in their success, you earn more than just their business—you earn their loyalty. You become the go-to person they rely on because they know you will always have their best interests at heart.

This doesn't mean being "perfect" or always offering the cheapest or most cutting-edge products; it means caring about their needs and showing them that you're committed to finding the right solutions for them—time and time again.

Being proactive and anticipating your client's needs is another critical aspect of providing value. Sometimes the best way to help your client is by solving a problem before they even realize it exists.

Whether it's offering an early solution to a challenge or suggesting a product that will streamline their processes, proactive sales show that you're thinking ahead, always keeping their success top of mind.

Responsiveness: Always Be There When They Need You

Being responsive is about more than just answering calls or emails promptly. It's about being there when your clients need you the most—whether it's for a small question or a big issue.

If something goes wrong, how you handle it can define the future of your relationship. Responding quickly, with empathy and a clear plan of action, shows your client that their needs matter to you—and that you'll be there to help them through any situation.

Maintaining a healthy and open communication channel, demonstrates your commitment to their success.

This level of responsiveness builds confidence and reassures clients that they're not just a number on your sales report—they're a partner you're invested in. Clients want to feel that they can depend on you not just for solutions but for support when things get tough.

Going above and beyond for your clients not only strengthens the relationship but also sets you apart from competitors. Make them feel that you feel for their project and success as if it were yours.

Building Relationships That Last

Relationship building in sales is not just about closing deals or hitting quotas. It's about creating lasting connections that grow over time. It's about trust, communication, and always putting the client's needs at the center of what you do.

The more you invest in these relationships, the more they'll invest in you. And when you consistently show up for your clients—when you listen, understand, deliver value, and stay responsive—you create a partnership that stands the test of time.

When you become the "go-to person" for your clients, they will not only stay loyal—they will become advocates, referring you to others and ensuring your long-term success. Relationships are the true currency of business, and the more you nurture them, the more your business will thrive.

So, take the time to build genuine relationships, invest in your clients' success, and treat them with the same care and respect you would a close friend. In doing so, you'll find that your business grows not just through one-off sales but through loyal, long-term partnerships that will stand strong for decades to come.

I remember when Argentina's economy started to decline. At that time, I was working with a SaaS company—Software as a Service—that did business there. We knew the situation was unsustainable, and many companies that relied on international trade were at risk of going bankrupt. We anticipated the challenges ahead and prepared several options to help our clients continue working with us.

We then proactively reached out to our clients, asking them to meet and discuss how we could plan for the future together. They were very grateful. Most of them opened up to us, sharing not only the current state of their businesses but also their fears and challenges. This helped us keep operations running despite the difficult circumstances and, more importantly, built a much stronger bond with them.

Chapter 5

Effective Communication Strategies

In sales, communication is everything. It's the difference between securing a deal and losing out on the opportunity of a lifetime. Mastering the art of effective communication can help you engage with clients, address their concerns, and close more deals. Let's explore the key strategies for effective communication in sales—clear and concise communication, answering the questions asked, active listening, and addressing client concerns and objections.

Clear and Concise Communication

One of the fundamental aspects of effective communication in sales is clarity. When speaking to clients, always aim to be clear and to the point. Avoid industry jargon or technical terms that might confuse or overwhelm your prospect. Instead, focus on communicating the benefits of your product or service in simple, straightforward language. Make it easy for the client to understand how your solution can solve their problems.

As the saying goes, "If you can't explain it simply, you don't understand it well enough."

Being clear doesn't mean dumbing down your language, but it does mean choosing simplicity over complexity. Sure, you may know all the technical terms and professional jargon in your field, but your goal isn't to impress your client with what you know—it's to help them understand how your offering will meet their needs. Save those complex terms for when the context demands it; for now, keep it super simple.

Clients appreciate an approachable, transparent salesperson who can break down information in an easy-to-understand way. This builds trust and ensures that your message isn't lost in translation.

Answer What You Were Asked

When engaging with a potential client, it is critical to actively listen to their needs and concerns. A successful sales interaction is one where you not only hear their questions but also understand the underlying issues they are trying to solve.

Your ability to respond directly to their inquiries with relevant, tailored information will significantly impact the way they perceive your solution. Avoid veering off onto tangents or providing extraneous details that may cloud the conversation or overwhelm the client. By addressing only what was asked, you demonstrate attentiveness and show that you're focused on delivering a solution that precisely meets their needs.

Keep in mind that clients move through different decision stages, and the level of detail you provide should match where they are on their journey. Understanding these stages will help you determine the depth and type of information to share, ensuring you remain aligned with their decision-making process.

The Three Decision Stages

1. Discovery Stage: At this stage, the client is in the process of gathering information and beginning to define their needs. They are not yet ready to dive into the specifics but are exploring solutions to their pain points. Your role here is to listen carefully, identify their core challenges, and offer high-level insights into how your product or service could address those challenges. Focus on building rapport and positioning yourself as a trusted advisor rather than getting into the weeds of your offering's features. At this stage, your communication should be more about exploration and relationship building than hard selling.

2. Consideration Stage: At this stage, the client is evaluating their options in more detail. They are no longer just gathering general information—they are now comparing

various solutions to determine which best fits their needs. This is the time to present more in-depth information that directly addresses the client's specific concerns and objectives.

You can share relevant case studies, data, and detailed use cases that demonstrate the effectiveness of your solution in scenarios similar to theirs.

However, be careful not to overwhelm the client with excessive information; focus on what is most pertinent to their current evaluation. Answer their questions thoroughly and ensure you are consistently aligning your response to the problems they've highlighted.

3. Decision Stage: At this stage, the client is close to making a purchase decision, and your role is to reassure them that they are making the right choice. They will likely

have final questions about the specifics of your product or service, including pricing, terms, implementation, or support.

Your answers should be clear, concise, and designed to reinforce the value and benefits of your offering. This is where you emphasize the unique selling points that distinguish your solution from others, whether it's return on investment, ease of implementation, superior customer service, or long-term value.

Ensure you address any remaining objections and ensure the client feels confident in their decision to move forward with your offering.

The Three Key Moments of the Sales Process

In addition to understanding the decision stages, it's essential to recognize the three critical moments in the sales process, where your approach to communication and information-sharing will vary.

1. The "Falling" Moment: The first moment you want to create is when the client falls in love with your product or service. At this stage, the client should begin to envision how your solution could fit into their operations and improve their situation. Your goal is to highlight the most compelling aspects of your product—its core capabilities, unique features, and the specific ways it can address the client's needs.

   Avoid getting into technical details or training content at this stage, as the objective is not to educate them fully about every function but rather to engage them emotionally and intellectually.

The key is to help them picture the outcome they desire—whether that's a smoother process, increased efficiency, or better results—and to show how your product can help them achieve it.

2. The "Setting the Rules" Moment: After you've captured the client's interest, it's time to establish clear expectations and guidelines.

This is a crucial moment for transparency and trust building. You must ensure that the client understands the terms and conditions of the sale as well as any limitations of the product or service.

However, it's important to communicate these details in a way that doesn't undermine the value of your offering. Avoid using negative language that may diminish the client's excitement. Instead, frame limitations in a positive, constructive manner.

For example:

Instead of saying, "We charge extra for every change you make," say, "Changes are allowed for an additional fee."

Rather than saying, "Adults pay more than children," try, "Children enjoy a discounted tariff."

Instead of saying, "You can only use the service during restricted hours," say, "You have flexibility in choosing when to access the service, Monday to Friday, between 9 a.m. and 5 p.m."

Instead of saying, "Pets are allowed only in small sizes," say, "We welcome small pets."

Always aim to frame conditions positively and use "AND" instead of "BUT" when possible to maintain an open, solutions-oriented conversation.

For example:

"Additional students are welcome, and you will only need to pay for their study material."

At this stage, clarity is key. You should avoid over-romanticizing your offer and instead be direct about what's possible and what's not. Resist the urge to dive into overly technical descriptions of every feature unless absolutely necessary for the client to understand how your product will fit into their business.

3. The "Training" Moment (if applicable): If your product or service requires training, the final moment comes after the deal has been closed. This is when you can get into

the nitty-gritty details of how to use the product or service effectively.

For many businesses, training is a separate process that requires in-depth knowledge, and often there are specialized teams to handle this. However, if you're a solo entrepreneur or part of a smaller team, you may be the one responsible for training.

The key during this phase is to ensure the client feels empowered and confident in their ability to use your product or service.

***

Bonus Tip: *When delivering training, always incorporate positive adjectives and emphasize the tools or features that will provide the most immediate value to the client.*

Highlight those capabilities that will help them avoid problems, solve existing issues, or drive success from day one.

This positive reinforcement will help the client feel more confident about their investment, strengthening the relationship and ensuring long-term satisfaction with your solution.

Active Listening in Conversations

As stated before, active listening is one of the most powerful tools in the toolkit of sales communication. It goes beyond simply hearing the words the client says—it's about fully engaging with them, understanding their perspective, and responding in a way that acknowledges both their words and underlying feelings.

When you practice active listening, you're not just hearing a potential client's concerns; it involves fully concentrating on what the client is saying, understanding their perspective, and responding thoughtfully.

To practice active listening effectively, use techniques that encourage engagement and demonstrate attentiveness. Maintain consistent eye contact to show you're focused, nod in agreement to signal that you're following the conversation, and ask clarifying questions when necessary to ensure you fully understand their needs. By doing so, you build rapport and show that you value what they are saying.

But active listening isn't just about passively absorbing information; it's an active process. It means asking the right questions to uncover the full picture of your client's needs and challenges. By digging deeper with thoughtful questions, you not only understand their immediate concerns but also identify any potential future needs or underlying pain points that may not be obvious at first glance.

This approach will help you tailor your responses more accurately and set you up to provide a truly relevant and impactful proposal when the time comes.

Addressing Client Concerns and Objections

In any sales process, client concerns or objections are inevitable. These are natural reactions that reflect the client's desire to ensure they are making the right decision. It's vital to approach these objections with empathy and understanding rather than dismissing them. By acknowledging their concerns sincerely, you validate their feelings and demonstrate that you respect their decision-making process.

Address objections head-on with thoughtful responses that not only acknowledge the client's concerns but also highlight the strengths of your offering in relation to those concerns. For instance, if a client is concerned about the price of your product, frame your response by highlighting the value it delivers—such as the long-term cost savings, unique features, or exceptional customer service that make the investment worthwhile.

However, it's essential to be honest and transparent about the capabilities of your product or service. Overpromising and under-delivering will only damage your credibility and create future problems. You must manage the client's expectations realistically to avoid any disappointments after the sale is made.

By proactively addressing concerns with clear, fact-based information, you demonstrate a commitment to meeting their needs and building a long-lasting relationship based on trust.

Effective Communication and Managing Client Expectations

Clear, transparent, and honest communication is critical in managing client expectations throughout the consultative sales process. It's not enough to simply talk about your product's features—you must also be upfront about what your product can and can't do and what the client can expect throughout the implementation and beyond.

Be transparent about what you can deliver, and set realistic goals with your clients.

As mentioned before, one key aspect of managing expectations is avoiding overpromising. When you set expectations that are too high, you risk under-delivering, which can harm both your relationship with the client and your reputation in the marketplace.

Instead, focus on being realistic and clear about the scope of your offering, the timeline for delivery, and any limitations or conditions that may apply. Setting clear goals from the outset and keeping clients informed every step of the way builds trust and creates a sense of partnership, making them more likely to remain loyal customers and fostering long-term relationships based on mutual understanding.

Speaking Positively to Influence Client Mindset

As we discussed earlier in the context of setting the rules, speaking positively is a crucial aspect of effective communication in sales.

When discussing your product or addressing a client's concerns, always frame your language in a positive, affirmative light. The way you phrase your communication shapes the client's perception of both you and your offering.

A positive tone not only influences the client's emotional response but also fosters a more productive, optimistic conversation.

For example:

Instead of saying, "They only come in black or silver," try saying, "They are part of our exclusive black-and-silver line."

Rather than saying, "We don't have physical offices; we only have home offices," say, "We are a virtual company that operates from various locations, embracing a work-from-home culture."

Instead of stating, "You will only have three reschedule opportunities for your appointments," say, "We offer flexibility and understand plans change, so we're including up to three free reschedule opportunities for your convenience."

In each case, the positive framing not only communicates the same information but also positions the offering in a more favorable light, making the client feel more positive about what they're receiving.

Proactively Handling Objections

One of the most effective ways to handle objections is to truly listen—not just to the words the client is saying but to the feelings and underlying concerns behind those words.

A common error for salespeople is to assume they know what the client needs based on their own experiences or biases. Instead, you should triangulate objections by seeking clarification, gathering additional perspectives, and making sure that you truly understand the client's unique situation.

Anticipate common objections based on your experience with other clients, but always approach each objection with the understanding that it's specific to that client's unique circumstances.

Reframe objections into questions that can help guide the conversation toward a solution. This strategy not only helps you uncover deeper insights but also allows you to position your product or service in the best possible light.

For example, if a client raises an objection about the price, rather than immediately defending the cost, ask questions like, "Can you tell me more about your budget concerns?" or "What features or benefits are most important to you?"

This gives you a clearer picture of their priorities and allows you to respond to their concerns more directly while also strengthening your relationship by demonstrating that you genuinely care about their needs.

Using Proof Points to Strengthen Your Position

When addressing objections, one of the most effective ways to build credibility and trust is to provide proof points—real-world examples, case studies, testimonials, or data that demonstrate the value of your product or service.

These proof points allow the client to see that others have faced similar challenges and have successfully used your product or service to overcome them.

Additionally, it's important to focus on value over price. While price is a key factor in any sales decision, clients are often more willing to pay a premium if they see clear, tangible value. Focus on the long-term benefits your solution provides—whether it's increased efficiency, time saved, or improved outcomes—and use examples to help them visualize how they'll benefit from working with you.

Building Trust Early and Guiding the Decision-Making Process

The best salespeople understand that the goal is not to push for a quick sale but to build trust and guide the client through their decision-making process.

This means offering all viable options transparently and helping the client make the most informed choice based on their needs. Rather than hard-selling your product, take the time to listen and educate, answering questions honestly and offering solutions that are in the client's best interest.

When you take a consultative approach to sales—focusing on helping the client make the right choice, not just closing the deal—you build a stronger, more trusting relationship. Clients will appreciate your honesty and feel more comfortable moving forward with a decision that aligns with their true needs.

In conclusion, mastering the art of effective communication in sales is essential for creating strong, long-lasting client relationships and closing deals successfully. By practicing active listening, addressing client concerns with empathy, speaking positively, and setting realistic expectations, you can enhance your sales skills and position yourself as a trusted advisor.

Building trust early in the sales process, addressing objections proactively, and guiding the client to a well-informed decision will not only help you close more deals but will also set the foundation for ongoing, successful client partnerships.

By implementing these strategies, you can build a solid reputation, increase client satisfaction, and achieve greater success in your sales career.

Chapter 6

Building a Healthy Pipeline: The Key to Sustainable Sales Success

The relationship is the human part of the equation, but let's not forget that, at its core, sales is also about numbers. To achieve the right results, you need the right numbers in your pipeline. A consistent and healthy sales pipeline doesn't just guarantee your success; it's the engine that drives your revenue and sustainable growth.

In this chapter, we'll explore the importance of building and maintaining a healthy pipeline and provide practical tips for sales professionals to optimize their pipeline management strategies.

Why Does a Healthy Pipeline Matter?

A healthy pipeline is absolutely critical for sales professionals to consistently meet their targets and fuel long-term business growth. It's not just a series of steps to follow; it's a well-structured pathway that empowers you to manage your sales process with intention and purpose.

One of the most important things to remember is that you own your sales process. If you fail to take charge of it, it will take charge of you. Without control over your pipeline, you lose the ability to predict outcomes, manage your goals effectively, and drive your sales efforts forward with confidence.

During sales meetings, I often hear responses like, "I'm thinking I should call again to see if...," "Maybe next month," "They didn't tell me," or "I don't know when..." When I hear these kinds of answers, I always ask my team one simple question: "Who is piloting the ship?" The reason I ask this is to remind them that your sales pipeline is like a ship, and it's your responsibility to steer it in the direction of success. The destination you're aiming for—meeting your goals, achieving sales targets, and driving revenue—can only be reached if you are the one at the helm, guiding the process.

Directing the wheel means taking full ownership of your pipeline. This involves setting specific, measurable commitments with your clients, establishing clear timelines, and creating an organized, transparent communication plan that moves the sales process forward. It's about being proactive rather than reactive, ensuring that every step you take is intentional and focused on achieving a successful outcome.

By constantly filling your pipeline with well-qualified leads and viable opportunities, you ensure a steady flow of potential clients. This proactive approach allows you to maintain consistent revenue and significantly reduce the impact of market fluctuations, seasonal trends, or unexpected changes.

A robust pipeline serves as a safety net, providing a reliable stream of prospects that you can engage with, nurture, and ultimately convert into loyal customers.

More than just a collection of names and contacts, a healthy pipeline provides sales professionals with the security and confidence they need to excel.

When you know that your pipeline is full of high-quality opportunities, you're better positioned to handle challenges, meet targets, and deliver results consistently. It's this sense of control and foresight that enables top performers to stay focused, resilient, and effective, no matter what the market throws their way.

Key Elements of a Healthy Pipeline

1. Consistent Lead Generation

One of the cornerstones of a healthy sales pipeline is consistent and proactive lead generation. As a sales professional, it's crucial to prioritize the continual creation of new leads to keep your pipeline full and vibrant. This means embracing creativity and thinking outside the box. Explore various channels, such as social media, networking events, online communities, and referrals, to attract fresh prospects.

Waiting for prospects to knock on your door simply isn't enough in today's fast-paced sales environment. You need to actively seek out opportunities. Attend events, engage in conversations, and surround yourself with your target audience. By immersing yourself in the right circles, you make it easier to establish relationships and be seen as an active and valuable option for them.

It's also important to note that cold-calling 50 people doesn't have the same impact as engaging with 50 individuals you've already interacted with, either in person or online. The difference is in the relationship you've built.

When you've established rapport and credibility, your outreach becomes much more effective.

2. Qualification and Prioritization

Not all leads are created equal. For a pipeline to be truly healthy, it must be filled with the right kinds of opportunities. Sales professionals should focus on qualifying leads by evaluating key factors such as budget, timeline, needs, and overall fit with your product or service. This ensures you're investing your time and resources in the most promising prospects.

As we discussed in Chapter 2, there are processes for properly qualifying opportunities. Use them to cleanse your pipeline by ensuring that you're only pursuing leads that are worth your time. Prioritize them effectively, deciding who to focus on first and how much attention each deal requires. This allows you to allocate your resources where they matter most.

Remember, as we've previously mentioned, everyone is a buyer, but not everyone is your buyer. The numbers won't lie—qualify your opportunities to stay realistic and focused. Don't be afraid to let go of deals that are no longer moving forward or that aren't progressing in a meaningful way.

3. Effective Follow-Up

Effective and timely follow-up is key to maintaining momentum in your sales process. A lead may not be ready to make a purchase on your first conversation, but consistent, personalized follow-up will keep the relationship alive and move them closer to a decision.

It's important to nurture leads through regular communication, addressing their questions, concerns, and objections. Always offer value in your follow-up by providing relevant content, insights, or resources that help keep the prospect engaged. This approach ensures that when they're ready to make a decision, you remain top of mind.

4. Pipeline Visibility and Tracking

It's impossible to manage a pipeline effectively without complete visibility into its status at all times. Sales professionals need to stay organized and aware of the state of every opportunity they're working on.

This is where CRM tools and dashboards become essential. These tools allow sales teams to track leads, opportunities, and sales activities in real time, helping to identify bottlenecks and prioritize tasks. By analyzing this data, sales professionals can make data-driven decisions that optimize their pipeline performance. Regular tracking ensures that you stay on top of your sales goals and can adjust your approach as needed to improve results.

5. Continuous Adaptation

The sales landscape is always shifting. Market conditions, customer preferences, and competitor actions evolve constantly, which means sales professionals must be flexible and adaptable. Those who can't pivot risk falling behind.

To maintain a healthy pipeline, it's essential to stay informed about changes in the economy, industry trends, and emerging developments.

Learning from past successes and failures can provide invaluable insights into what strategies work and what needs improvement. By consistently refining your sales strategies based on up-to-date information, you position yourself to stay ahead of the competition.

Building a healthy pipeline requires continuous adaptation. Adapt not only to external factors but also to the feedback you receive from prospects and customers. This approach ensures that your pipeline remains robust, dynamic, and responsive to the ever-changing market.

6. Understanding the Silent "No"

In consultative selling, it's natural to encounter a range of responses throughout the sales cycle—from objections to questions about product features. However, the challenge often lies in recognizing when a prospect has quietly disengaged, even if they haven't overtly said "no."

Understanding the silent "no" is crucial to maintaining a healthy pipeline. Many prospects won't reject you outright but will instead exhibit signs of disinterest in subtle ways. Recognizing these signals early helps you avoid wasting time on opportunities that aren't going to close.

There are several types of silent "no" responses:

- Etiquette and Evasion: Some prospects prefer to avoid confrontation and will politely delay or defer decisions. They might say things like "I'll consider it," "Let me think about it," or "Can we revisit this next month?"

While these phrases may seem neutral, they are often a form of rejection. It's important to recognize this and not chase them indefinitely.

- Genuine Interest, But Not Now: A prospect may have real interest in your offering but requires additional time to evaluate it or consult with others. They may say things like, "I need to talk to my team" or "Let's revisit this next quarter." If you hear these kinds of responses multiple times, it's likely a subtle "no." My suggestion: Assume it's a temporal loss, enroll the contact in a nurturing campaign, and book a re-approaching call for the season or future date they suggest the project may resume.

- Reservations and Objections: Sometimes prospects voice objections, such as concerns about pricing or product fit. These objections can be addressed, and with the right approach, you may be able to turn them into an opportunity. But, if after addressing the objection the prospect continues to hesitate, it's time to reconsider whether they're truly a buyer.

- Miscommunication or Ambiguity: At times, what appears to be a rejection might actually be due to a misunderstanding or unclear communication about the prospect's needs. If you've clarified the issues but still don't see movement, it's likely that the prospect is not ready to proceed.

- Competing Priorities: Prospects may genuinely be interested but have more pressing priorities that prevent them from committing right now. In this case, it's crucial to acknowledge that there is no immediate opportunity and leave the door open for future conversations.

The key to recognizing these subtle "no" signals is to remain observant and sensitive to the prospect's language, tone, and behavior. Discerning these reactions allows you to focus your energy and time on the leads that are truly worth pursuing and not waste resources chasing deals that are unlikely to close.

***

My bonus tip: *When in doubt, like in baseball, three strikes and you're out.*

If you feel that a prospect is consistently delaying their decision, consider using the three strikes rule:
1. *First attempt: Reach out and accept the delay while setting a specific date to follow up.*
2. *Second attempt: Follow up on the agreed-upon date and be more direct. If they delay again, suggest one last follow-up to hear their final decision.*
3. *Third attempt: If the delay continues, politely inform the prospect that you will respect their timeline, but should they decide to move forward, you'll be ready. Leave your contact details and express your willingness to reconnect when they are ready.*

This approach allows you to maintain professionalism, keep the door open, and ultimately move on if the deal is not progressing.

7. Seeking Feedback and Learning from Mistakes: Embracing a Growth Mindset

Losing a client to a competitor is always a tough experience, but it's also an opportunity for growth. Every loss offers valuable lessons that can strengthen your sales approach and make you more effective in the future. The key is to handle the situation with grace and a growth mindset.

- Acceptance and Professionalism: When you lose a client, always accept the decision with professionalism. Reacting emotionally or defensively will only harm the relationship and make it harder to work with the client in the future.

- Request Feedback: Once the loss is acknowledged, reach out to the client for feedback. This can be done through email, phone, or even a face-to-face meeting, depending on the nature of the relationship.

Ask open-ended questions like:
➡ What factors influenced your decision?
➡ Were there areas where we could have offered more value?
➡ What did you like most about our proposal? What did you like least?

Active listening is essential here. Be attentive and show that you value their feedback, even if it's difficult to hear. Do not interrupt or argue —simply listen and understand.

* Analyze and Learn: Take the feedback seriously and look for patterns. What recurring issues or objections came up? This analysis will help you identify areas for improvement, both personally and within your sales process.

- Make Strategic Adjustments: Based on the feedback, make necessary adjustments to your sales approach. Work with your team to address any gaps or weaknesses in your offerings. Focus on continuous improvement, but also be realistic about what you can and cannot change.

- Seek Training and Development: If the feedback points to gaps in your skills or knowledge, take steps to improve. This might involve further training, product knowledge, or refining your interpersonal skills.

- Maintain Relationships: Even after losing a client, it's important to nurture the relationship. Keep them updated on any changes or improvements, and remain open to future opportunities. If you have a marketing team, work together to ensure your brand stays visible without being intrusive.

- Share the Lessons Learned: Finally, share your experiences and lessons with your sales team. By doing so, you foster a culture of continuous improvement and help everyone learn from both successes and failures.

Chapter 7

From Overcoming Challenges in Consultative Sales to Building Long-Term Relationships

Consultative sales can be incredibly rewarding, but it's also a field filled with challenges. Many sales professionals may claim to be consultants yet continue to use generic, "one-size-fits-all" pitches that resemble scripts used by call centers. These individuals might succeed in the short term by convincing customers to make a one-off purchase, but they often struggle with repeat business. Their success is dependent on their ability to acquire new one-time buyers, and when this pipeline slows, so does their income.

In contrast, the true consultative sales professional doesn't just close a sale—they deliver structured solutions that lead to well-implemented projects that are renewed over time. This process creates a steady, cumulative income stream that grows year after year. If you find yourself in this position, congratulations—you're on the right track for a successful career in sales. But don't stop there; you can take it one step further.

In this section, we'll explore not only how to overcome the common obstacles faced by consultative sales professionals—such as rejection, managing client expectations, and handling difficult conversations—but also how to cultivate a belief in your own abilities. This is a process of growth, one that can sometimes be painful, exhausting, and stressful, but is ultimately always rewarding.

Dealing with Rejection and Overcoming Obstacles

One of the greatest challenges in consultative sales is handling rejection and overcoming obstacles. It's crucial to remember that rejection is not a reflection of your value as a consultant or a salesperson. Rather, rejection is an inherent part of the sales process, a step toward improvement. View each "no" as an opportunity to refine your approach, adjust your pitch, and grow in your role.

Becoming a seasoned and mature sales professional means understanding that not every prospect will convert into a client. Not every interaction will result in a sale. However, each encounter is an important data point, and over time, your success will be a product of these cumulative experiences. Sales are essentially a numbers game: the more opportunities you engage with, the higher your probability of success. So, remember, every "no" you receive brings you one step closer to a "yes."

Handling Difficult Conversations with Confidence

Difficult conversations are an inevitable part of consultative sales, whether you're negotiating terms, addressing client concerns, setting expectations, or delivering difficult news. When faced with these challenges, it's vital to approach the conversation with empathy, active listening, and a solutions-oriented mindset.

Stay calm and focused, and remember that your goal is not to defend yourself or your position but to understand the client's needs and find a mutually beneficial solution. It's about focusing on the client and their needs, not on your ego, anxiety to close the deal, or fear of rejection.

By handling difficult conversations professionally and with grace, you will not only resolve the issue at hand but also strengthen your relationship with the client. This will position you as someone who can navigate complex situations with skill and poise.

Truly Understanding Your Portfolio and the Value You Offer

In consultative sales, success hinges on your ability to deeply understand the products and services you offer as well as the value they provide to your clients. This understanding is foundational, as it allows you to communicate your offerings clearly and confidently to prospects.

Take the time to thoroughly familiarize yourself with your company's portfolio, its unique selling points, and the specific needs your services address. When you are genuinely knowledgeable, you can position yourself as a trusted advisor to your clients.

In the first chapters, we discussed the importance of knowing your catalog by heart. But this goes beyond just knowing your products—it's about understanding the broader picture, including your company's brand value. What is your company's reputation? How do clients perceive your brand? Do you know how your offerings are positioned in the market and how they compare to competitors' products and services?

By gaining a solid grasp of your own market position, you empower yourself to make better pricing decisions and to negotiate more effectively. Your understanding of your company's brand value will guide how you approach stakeholders, competitors, suppliers, and, of course, clients.

When you own your position in the market, it becomes easier to act with confidence and communicate your value.

The Real-Life Example of a Sales Rep Who Learned the Hard Way:

Several years ago, I worked with a sales representative who was particularly fond of one product in the portfolio. She felt comfortable with it, and it became the focus of nearly every pitch she made.

Initially, her sales were strong because she used traditional, convincing techniques that worked for a while. However, over time, as the rest of the sales team grew in terms of repeat sales and expanding client bases, her customer list began to shrink, and her income stagnated.

Why? Because she was trying to force-fit every client into the same solution, much like forcing Cinderella's slipper onto every foot, regardless of size or shape. Not every client is suited to the same solution. What worked in the beginning couldn't sustain long-term growth.

This is a powerful lesson: convincing every client that a single product fits all needs is not the same as addressing their specific requirements. In consultative sales, it's about listening to your clients, identifying their needs, answering what needs to be clarified, and offering the solution that is the best fit for them, not the one you're most comfortable with.

Overcoming Challenges in Consultative Sales: A Summary

Overcoming challenges in consultative sales requires a unique combination of skills: resilience, self-awareness, effective communication, empathy, and a deep understanding of your portfolio and value proposition. The road to success is not always smooth, and you will inevitably face rejection, difficult conversations, and client objections. However, by continuously learning and refining your approach, you can build stronger relationships and secure long-term, repeat business.

Ultimately, the true beauty of consultative sales lies in building lasting, mutually beneficial relationships. By focusing on the client's needs and consistently offering value, you'll be able to transform one-time buyers into loyal customers who will continue to engage with you—and grow your income year after year.

By moving from overcoming challenges to building these enduring relationships, you position yourself as a trusted advisor, not just a salesperson. This is the foundation for long-term success in the consultative sales world. Keep learning, keep evolving, and always be willing to grow alongside your clients. That's the key to sustainable, fulfilling success in sales.

Chapter 8

Closing

Closing a sale is often viewed as the final hurdle in the sales process. However, it's actually the culmination of the trust, rapport, and alignment you've built with the client throughout your interactions.

The key to successfully closing lies in the questions you ask and the manner in which you guide the conversation. A skilled salesperson understands that, while the closing stage may seem like the end, it is, in reality, just another step in a larger process that fosters long-term relationships and repeat business.

Using the Right Type of Questions

One of the most powerful tools in the consultative sales process is the art of asking the right questions. These questions should be thoughtfully designed to uncover the prospect's needs, motivations, and pain points—allowing you to craft a tailored solution.

Initially, exploratory questions are incredibly effective in this phase. These are open-ended questions that prompt the prospect to reveal information beyond simple yes or no answers. Open-ended inquiries allow you to gain deeper insights into the client's true needs and preferences, which sets the stage for a consultative approach.

For example, when you ask, "What challenges have you been facing in this area?" or "What would success look like for your team?" you are giving the prospect the opportunity to express their specific needs, which then helps you guide the conversation toward a more customized solution.

Open-ended questioning serves as the foundation for a consultative sales method, one that focuses on addressing the customer's circumstances and needs rather than just pushing a product. By positioning yourself as a trusted advisor rather than a traditional salesperson, you build a stronger rapport and instill confidence. These connections are vital in fostering long-term client relationships and ensuring future business.

However, when you move toward the closing stage, it is essential to transition from open-ended to leading questions. Leading questions are designed to guide the prospect toward a specific answer, thereby helping you maintain control of the conversation and guide them toward a commitment.

Leading Questions: Maintaining Control at the Close

Leading questions subtly direct the prospect toward a particular conclusion. They suggest an answer within the question itself, creating a clear path toward closing the deal. These questions help ensure the conversation moves forward, and they guide the prospect to visualize the benefits of your offer.

For example:

➡Which option do you prefer: A or B?
➡Based on your needs, which solution makes the most sense for your team?
➡Do you think it would be more beneficial to go with the option that covers all your requirements or the one that offers additional value?
➡Given your timeline, which of these options would be the best fit for your organization?

The goal with leading questions is to keep the momentum going while helping the client clearly see how your solution fits into their needs and objectives. It's essential to prepare and practice these questions beforehand so you can navigate the conversation smoothly and be ready to handle any unexpected responses that may arise.

The 4Ps: Present, Prompt, Provoke, and Pressure

A successful close relies not only on effective questioning but also on a systematic approach to the conversation. A strategy I've found highly effective is the 4P method for closing: Present, Prompt, Provoke, and Pressure.

1. **Present**: Start by clearly presenting the solution or product that has been tailored to the client's needs. This isn't just about showcasing the features; it's about framing it in the context of how it will solve their unique challenges.

2. **Prompted Questions**: Use the prompted, almost "multiple-choice" style questions you've prepared to guide the prospect toward a decision. These questions should be designed to highlight the fit and benefits of your proposal in a way that makes the

prospect feel as though this is their project —not just your sale.

The more you align the solution with the client's vision, the more ownership they will feel over the decision.

3. **Provoke a Commitment**: The next step is to provoke a commitment by agreeing on the next steps. This should involve setting clear dates and actions that define the path forward, ensuring both parties are aligned on the project's launch or implementation.

This step shifts the focus from a simple purchase transaction to a more consultative, service-oriented mindset. It's no longer just about making a sale; it's about collaboratively setting the project in motion.

4. **Pressure = Power and Control**: Pressure is a natural part of the closing process, but it

should never feel like desperation. The key is to create a sense of urgency based on the client's own needs and timeline.

For example, if the client needs to deploy a solution by a certain date or achieve a specific goal, help them recognize the steps necessary to reach that objective. This shifts the narrative from "I need you to buy" to "I'm here to help you achieve your goals on time."

Depending on the circumstances, you can also use time-limited offers as a strategic way to encourage a decision. I personally prefer to offer added value rather than discounts. For instance, I'd rather say, "If you book by Friday, we'll include all meals for the trip," rather than "You'll get a 10% discount if you book by Friday."

Discounts can often diminish the perceived value of your product, and customers may feel disappointed if they don't act on the offer or assume that the product is overpriced. Instead, adding value creates a sense of exclusivity and reinforces the quality of your offer.

Maintaining Integrity and Trust

While closing the sale is a critical moment in the process, maintaining trust and integrity is even more important. The foundation of every sale is built on your reputation, and it's essential to honor your commitments and respect your client's confidentiality.

Never promise something you can't deliver, and always ensure that what you're offering is genuinely suited to the client's needs. A "bad sale"—where the customer is sold something that doesn't meet their needs or expectations—often leads to dissatisfaction and, worse, negative word of mouth. A dissatisfied customer is unlikely to return for repeat business and may even share their bad experience, which could hurt your reputation and future opportunities.

It's always better to secure a moderate sale that leads to repeat business over time than to win a one-time deal that ultimately feeds your competitors' client base.

Remember:
I may have lost a deal, but I cannot afford to lose a client.

The relationships you build in the sales process are far more valuable in the long term than any single transaction. Even if you don't close the deal now, maintaining a respectful, professional demeanor leaves the door open for future opportunities. Being polite, respectful, and responsive ensures that, when the client is ready to buy, they will turn to you first.

The art of closing a sale is not about pressure or manipulation; it's about providing value, guiding the client toward a solution that meets their needs, and building a long-term relationship based on trust and respect.

By using the right questions, maintaining control of the conversation, and closing with integrity, you'll not only secure the sale but also set the stage for continued success and repeat business.

In the end, closing is about helping your client make a decision that benefits them. If you can master this balance, you'll find that the sales process becomes smoother, and your relationships with clients will grow deeper, more meaningful, and more profitable.

Chapter 9

What Makes You Good

Becoming a successful salesperson is about more than just mastering techniques—it's about embodying the right mindset, building meaningful relationships, and continuously improving your craft.

Salespeople who excel are those who understand the key elements of their role and approach each step with dedication, discipline, and a consultative approach.

Getting to the Decision-Maker—Whoever They Are

One of the foundational aspects of sales is identifying and reaching the decision-makers within an organization. Don't be afraid to knock on doors, whether they are familiar or entirely new.

The "no" is already there, so the only real risk is being denied entry—an outcome that is inevitable for anyone who is hesitant to take action.

Whether you're working with a large corporation or a small startup, always be proactive and fearless in seeking out the right people.

Remember, the worst thing that can happen is a "no," and this only takes you one step closer to a "yes." Building the confidence to approach decision-makers directly will increase your chances of success and help you develop a more resilient sales strategy.

Knowing What You're Selling—Even If It's Not Your Expertise

As a salesperson, it's natural to feel that you might not be an expert in every field you sell within, but that shouldn't prevent you from becoming knowledgeable about what you're selling. It's vital to have a comprehensive understanding of the products or services you're representing, even if the field isn't your area of specialization.

You don't need to be an expert in every technical detail, but you should be able to answer common questions, outline the product's features and benefits, and understand its capabilities and limitations.

Ultimately, your role is to act as an advisor to your clients. Being well-versed in what you're selling allows you to communicate confidently and address any concerns, positioning yourself as a trusted resource for your clients.

Surround yourself with experts in the field, and continue learning. Over time, you will become the kind of consultant you would want to have if you were the client.

Doing the Right Follow-Up

Effective follow-up is a crucial aspect of the sales process that many professionals overlook or mishandle. As a sales consultant, knowing when and how to follow up is an essential skill that can significantly influence the outcome of a deal. Follow-up should never be an afterthought or something done out of routine. It must be strategic, timely, and aligned with the progression of the client's decision-making process.

In earlier chapters, we discussed the importance of setting clear agreements and timelines with your prospects. Staying organized and committed to these schedules demonstrates respect and professionalism. It also allows you to keep track of the negotiation's progress and engage with your clients at the right moments.

By maintaining an organized follow-up process, you foster more meaningful conversations that build trust and move the sales cycle forward.

Avoid generic follow-ups that don't add value; make sure your communications are specific, targeted, and relevant to the client's needs and stage in the buying process.

DO NOT IMPROVISE!

Being Able to Close the Deal

No matter how well you've executed every step of the sales process, if you can't close the deal, you're not truly performing the role of a salesperson. Closing is the ultimate goal of the sales journey, and the ability to convert prospects into clients is a defining characteristic of top-performing salespeople.

Many organizations have support teams—marketing, pre-sales, sales enablement, customer success, and post-sales support—that assist in the sales process. However, in today's fast-paced corporate environment, it's rare to find organizations with large teams handling the pre-sale activities. More often, salespeople are expected to take on a variety of responsibilities, from lead generation to closing, as companies look to streamline operations and maximize individual performance.

It's important to recognize that your ability to close the deal directly impacts the success of your sales career. If you're not closing, you can't be considered a true sales professional. Again, master the art of closing, and you'll unlock the true potential of your sales career.

Chapter 10

What Makes You Unique

What separates top-tier salespeople from the rest? It's not just about the number of deals closed; it's about the qualities that distinguish you from the average salesperson.

Here are five key aspects that will help you stand out and thrive in the competitive world of sales:

1. Invest Your Time as if It Were Money —Because It Is!
2. Listen More Than You Talk —Don't Just Hear, Listen!
3. Make Sure Your Own Business Plan Is More Ambitious Than the One from the Company You Work For
4. Have a Relational Mindset
5. Act Now, Plan Long Term

1. Invest Your Time as if It Were Money—Because It Is

Time is the one resource that you can never get back. Just as you manage your financial resources carefully, you should treat your time with the same level of respect. Each minute spent on a deal should be viewed as an investment, and you need to be aware of how much time you are investing in each opportunity.

Take the time to calculate how much your time is worth—not just in terms of your fixed salary but including commissions, bonuses, and any other forms of compensation you receive. The more skilled and efficient you become, the more valuable your time becomes.

By recognizing your true time cost, you'll avoid wasting hours on prospects who aren't ready to buy or are not an ideal fit for your organization.

Use an opportunity qualification system to prioritize prospects based on their readiness and likelihood to close, ensuring that every minute you invest has the potential for significant returns.

2. Listen More Than You Talk—Don't Just Hear, Listen!

As I've emphasized repeatedly throughout this book, listening is one of the most powerful tools in sales. Seniority and success in sales aren't determined by how well you talk but by how well you listen. Understanding your client's needs is critical to crafting the right solution and ultimately winning the sale.

The key here is to listen actively—not to hear passively. Pay attention to the underlying concerns, motivations, and objectives of your clients. Tailor your responses to address their specific needs and challenges. Speak only when you have something valuable to add, ensuring that your discourse is concise, solution-oriented, and relevant to the client's situation.

This will not only help you win the sale but also earn the trust and respect of your clients, which is invaluable for building long-term relationships.

3. Make Sure Your Own Business Plan Is More Ambitious Than the One from the Company You Work For

Salespeople are often evaluated based on key performance indicators (KPIs) like sales volume, revenue, and conversion rates. While it's essential to understand your company's targets and compensation structure, the true secret to success is setting personal, ambitious goals that go beyond the company's expectations.

The most successful salespeople are those who use the company's goals as a baseline and then push themselves further to achieve more. Sales is one of the few professions where your income is directly tied to your effort and results. The harder you work, the greater your rewards.

This is one of the best-kept secrets and motivations behind why many people from diverse backgrounds stay in sales once they enter the field. While it's undoubtedly hard work, sales offers a unique opportunity: your financial success is entirely in your hands. Achieving your goals depends on your effort, meaning that it depends solely on you, so work toward the life you want!

By setting more ambitious goals for yourself, you'll not only exceed your company's expectations but also position yourself for professional growth and recognition.

When you surpass the standard targets, you build a reputation for excellence that will serve you throughout your career.

4. Have a Relational Mindset

The number of zeros on a salesperson's paycheck is directly proportional to the level of relationships and trust they are able to build in the market. The value of your network and reputation will often be the deciding factor in your career success. Mastering client relationships is crucial to ensuring that your sales pipeline stays full, year after year.

A strong reputation allows you to create a name for yourself in your industry. Being a trusted advisor, participating in industry conversations, and networking with key players helps you become more than just a salesperson—you become a businessperson.

Becoming a businessperson is not only about money, which in many cases places you at the top of the income ladder in the corporate world. It also unlocks the potential to propose and drive changes in processes, products, and even markets or industries.

A strong network and a solid reputation are assets that will help you weather tough times and generate new business opportunities. Just remember to nurture these relationships, but never take them for granted. Overuse or exploit your connections, and you risk damaging what you've worked hard to build.

5. Act Now, Plan Long Term

Before you can become a good leader, you need to understand the business at its core. There are few positions in an organization that give you as close an insight into its reality as sales.

Therefore, if you want to become a great sales director, you must be able to teach your team how to replicate your success. So, go out, sell, and become a salesperson worthy of being replicated.

Sales is a fast-paced environment, but it's also an area that offers tremendous opportunities for those who think long term. Whether you want to advance to a leadership position or build a sustainable career, developing a long-term mindset is key.

If you aspire to be a sales director or move into a C-level role, you need to understand the business from every angle. Take actionable steps every day toward your goal, and make decisions that align with your long-term vision.

Success in sales isn't just about immediate wins—it's about consistently putting in the work, learning from every experience, and building toward a bigger future.

Make plans for how much you want to earn and what you want to become, but start working toward it **now!**

* * *

Bonus Tip: *Once you begin to see significant earnings, don't immediately raise your standard of living. Open a separate savings account, and aim to have at least a year's worth of living expenses set aside. Manage your finances like you would manage a business, and always keep your future financial goals in mind.*

True success, whether measured in terms of income, career progression, or personal fulfillment, comes from consistently making smart decisions and behaving with discipline and foresight. By focusing on five areas—time management, listening skills, personal ambition, relationships, and long-term planning—you'll set yourself apart as a sales professional who excels, not just in the short term, but for the long haul.

And always allow yourself to feel and savor the sweet taste of success, whatever that means to you!

Appendix 1
Answers to Exercises

Chapter 2
Case A

Fact	Situation	Score
Size (DS)	Private university interested in 5,000 licenses	5
Decision-Maker (DM)	Procurement department	4
Need (N)	They are actively looking for licenses for their campus computers	5
Time (T)	They need them to be installed in less than two months	5
Budget (B)	There is a budget, but it is still unknown	3
TOTAL		**22**

Size, need, and time in this case are your best-case scenario, so they represent an obvious 5. The decision-maker, being an evident positive case, can be considered a 5 if in the conversation you found they are the one and only person to make the decision or a 4 if some other person or department may need to be involved; in many cases, procurement departments need a user area to approve or agree that the product to be acquired fully matches their needs.

On the other hand, the budget is a different story. Do we know what it is? No, we don't... so a 3 becomes the only option. If you got a total of 22 or 23, it is properly qualified, and you have an opportunity with an ideal client!

Case B

Fact	Situation	Score
Size (DS)	Company with 80 computers	1
Decision-Maker (DM)	Receptionist	1
Need (N)	We offer the software, and they seem to be interested	3
Time (T)	They do not have a clear purchasing date, but it may be in a year	1
Budget (B)	They do not have an assigned budget for the project, but it was said that they may take it from something else	2
TOTAL		**8**

For Case B, remember that the ideal deal size given is 5,000 units per purchase order. As 80 computers is not big enough to be considered positive and does not achieve even 5% of your ideal, then it's a minimum viable 1. Your point of contact is far from being part of the decision: 1. They "seem to be interested" is a visual perception, and objective qualifications only depend on what was said by our prospect or contact, so, not having been said, we do not know if there is a need or not: 3. The timeline is a year: 1. There is no budget, but it may be allocated by the client: 2.

If you got 8, it is properly qualified, and right now, there is not a real opportunity.

Appendix 2
Practical Applications of Consultation with Client-Centric Strategies

Here are some exercises that can be done to master your consultation skills focusing on a client's needs.

1. Create profiles of client needs, then analyze how your catalog can cover each profile needs and the products that can be a better fit. Focus on the client's needs, not on the organization's characteristics or name.

2. If you have recordings or transcripts of real meetings from past negotiations, review them from a neutral point of view. Then, create a questionnaire with what you think you need to ask; read/listen to the conversation again, looking for the answers; qualify the opportunity.

Assess if the time invested was in accordance with the qualifications obtained.

What product or service would you have offered with the current analysis?
Does it correspond to the one you presented at the time?

3. Go to your best success stories and make the analysis needs vs offered product, time invested vs qualification, frequency and type of contact vs your usual frequency and time for the similar kind of prospect.

4. If allowed, record your current meetings, and then listen to the conversation as a spectator and take new notes. Compare those with the notes you took during the meeting. Did they take you to the same conclusions? Did you miss or misunderstand something when you were with the client?

5. Use the recordings of your past first meetings or consultation meetings with clients, and make a focus and quality communication analysis. Who spoke more, the client or you? Did everything you said add value to the conversation, or did you use empty phrases? Was the client feeling understood? Did your comments make sense for the client? Were there uncomfortable silences? Was there a point when the conversation felt uneasy? Why?

6. Use the recordings of your past closing meetings and make an analysis. Who drove the conversation? What kinds of questions did you ask? If you were a third party, would you say it felt like a project conversation or like a sales transaction? How would you re-do it, if that were possible?

7. Take all the characteristics from your products and services and, instead of describing them, write them in terms of how they make the client's life or organization better.

   E.g. If you say, "It is small and light," you can say, "It is easy to carry and will fit into any bag you use."

   If you say, "It is tender and well seasoned," you can say, "You will find it delicious. It melts in your mouth."

Go Create Your Own Success Story!

I trust that your smart work will lead you to remarkable success.

Wish you all the best,

Sandra Rojas

www.ingramcontent.com/pod-product-compliance
Lightning Source LLC
LaVergne TN
LVHW051122080426
835510LV00018B/2193